Introduction

Gin, brandy, light and dark rum, whisky, North American bourbon and vodka are perfect basics to keep for mixing cocktails at home while fruit syrups, plus bitters like Angostura, make useful additions. Red grenadine syrup makes a great colour enhancer and Worcestershire Sauce is a necessity for drinks such as Bloody Mary. Keep a stock of soft drinks for topping up: cola, orange juice, ginger ale, tonic, mineral water and lemonade.

This edition published ... by Merehurst Limited
Ferry House ...
Putney, ...
Repri...

ISB...
A...
Designe...
Printe...
Distributed in the UK ...
9 Trinity Centre, Park Farm, Wellingb...
Distributed in Australia by J.B. Fairfax Press ...
80 McLachlan Avenue, Rushcutters Bay, Sydney, NSW 20...

Written By Tim Cole

Planter's Punch Royal

Makes 1 drink

From the Caribbean, this drink is based on rum and packed with fresh fruit.

½ lemon
1 lime
½ orange
1 tablespoon pineapple juice
4 tablespoons white rum
4 ice cubes
2 tablespoons dark rum

DECORATION
1 cocktail cherry
1 slice each lemon, lime and orange
Fresh mint leaves

EXTRAS
1 medium-sized tumbler
1 straw

1 Squeeze juice from lemon, lime and orange. Strain into a tumbler then stir in pineapple juice.

2 Add white rum and ice cubes, stirring until the glass appears to mist over. Mix in dark rum.

3 Decorate as shown in the picture with the cherry, fruit slices and mint leaves. Add a straw to the glass.

MIXER'S TIP
An exotic drink like Planter's Punch can afford to be lavishly decorated and a fun touch is to use 'stirrers' made from lengths of fresh, peeled pineapple. Each one should measure about 10cm (4in) in length by 2.5cm (1in) wide. Straws can then be an optional extra.

Planter's Punch Royal

Tequila Sunrise

Makes 1 drink

A classic favourite from Mexico.

3 tablespoons Tequila
250ml (8fl oz/1 cup) freshly-squeezed orange juice
4 ice cubes
1 tablespoon grenadine syrup

EXTRAS
1 cocktail or wine glass
An orange slice to decorate

1 Pour Tequila, orange juice and 2 ice cubes into a cocktail shaker or thermos flask. Shake gently for about 20 seconds.

2 Strain drink into glass through a sieve. Add remaining ice cubes.

3 Slowly pour the grenadine syrup into the glass and wait until it sinks to the bottom.

4 Immediately before serving, stir the drink from the centre to the outside edge. Decorate the glass with a slice of orange.

TIP
For a non-alcoholic version, use mineral water instead of Tequila, making it in exactly the same way.

TRENDY TEQUILA
Tequila is the national spirit of Mexico, distilled from the agave plant and completely colourless. It is booming in the west as a mixer drink though courageous drinkers might prefer it taken in Mexican fashion - neat! This is how: Put some salt on the back of your left hand. Hold the glass of Tequila in your right hand and pick up a slice of lemon with your left. Lick off the salt, throw back the Tequila and slowly suck the lemon. Deliciously refreshing, but not too many as Tequila has an unexpected kick!

Tequila Sunrise

Coffee Flip

Makes 1 drink

This cocktail is so luscious it is almost a dessert in a glass.

4 ice cubes
1 egg
1 teaspoon icing sugar or sugar syrup
2 teaspoons whipping cream
1 tablespoon brandy
1 tablespoon Tia Maria or Kahlua

DECORATION

Freshly grated nutmeg

EXTRAS

1 medium-sized cocktail glass, chilled beforehand
1 straw

1 Pour the ice cubes and egg into a cocktail shaker or thermos flask and shake briskly for 25 seconds.

2 Add all remaining ingredients. Cover and shake for 15 seconds.

3 Strain cocktail into glass through a fine sieve and sprinkle with nutmeg. Add the straw.

TO SHAKE OR TO STIR

Experienced bartenders, like magicians, make cocktail-making look the easiest thing in the world. You may not have the same confidence first time round but practice makes perfect. Just remember - drinks with fruit juice, sugar, eggs and/or cream are generally shaken in a shaker or whisked by hand before being strained into a glass. Others are gently stirred in the glass with a long-handled spoon.

Coffee Flip

Ice Cream Soda with Grenadine

Makes 1 drink

With or without alcohol, this is a wonderful cooling drink on hot summer days.

1 tablespoon grenadine syrup
Sparkling mineral water
1 tablespoon white rum
1 scoop of lemon sorbet or vanilla ice cream

DECORATION
1 cocktail cherry
5-6 fresh mint leaves

EXTRAS
1 large tumbler, chilled beforehand
1 straw

1 Pour grenadine into the prepared glass and add a splash of mineral water. Stir to mix and then add rum.

2 Add lemon sorbet or ice cream to the glass and then top up with mineral water. You can, if preferred, use sparkling white wine or grape juice instead of water.

3 Decorate with the cocktail cherry and mint leaves and then add a straw to the glass.

THE GREAT REFRESHER - ICED TEA
What do clever people drink on hot and humid days? The best thirst quencher of them all - iced tea. Here's how: Make very strong tea with about 10 tea bags and 1 litre (1¾ pints/4 cups) of boiling water. Brew as usual, leave until cold then strain into a large glass jug. Add another litre (1¾ pints/4 cups) chilled water. Sweeten to taste and add the juice of 1 lemon. Cover and chill in refrigerator. To serve, pour into tumblers over ice cubes (about 4 in each) and then add slices of lemon. Decorate with fresh mint leaves.

Ice Cream Soda with Grenadine

Morning Glory

Makes 1 drink

Cool, refreshing and silky smooth.

½ small Honeydew melon
Juice of 1 lime
3 tablespoons white rum
1 dash of cherry liqueur
4 ice cubes

DECORATION
¼ of an orange slice

EXTRAS
1 fairly large tumbler
1 straw

1 De-seed melon and then remove flesh with a spoon.

2 Put into a blender goblet with lime juice, rum, cherry liqueur and ice cubes and blend for about 20 seconds until a smooth purée.

3 Pour drink into the tumbler and then decorate glass with orange slice. Add a straw.

MIXER TIPS.
Long drinks taste best when made from fresh fruit juice, squeezed just before use if it's citrus, to retain its full flavour. When mixing drinks in general, pour fruit juice into the glass first, followed by alcohol. Bubbly drinks like sparkling mineral water keep their fizz if added last. When using slices or pieces of unpeeled citrus fruit, make sure the whole fruit is thoroughly washed in hot water to remove any chemical residue left after spraying.

Morning Glory

Rainbow Cocktail

Makes 1 drink

A feast for the eyes and quite potent!

3 medium oranges
½ lemon
4 ice cubes
3 tablespoons vodka
1½ tablespoons whipping cream
1 tablespoon blue curaçao
1 tablespoon grenadine syrup

DECORATION

1 cocktail cherry

EXTRAS

1 tall cocktail glass
1 cocktail stick
1 straw

1 Halve oranges and cut off 1 slice for decoration. Squeeze juice from oranges. Squeeze juice from lemon. Put juices into a cocktail shaker or thermos flask with ice cubes.

2 Add vodka and cream and shake for 20 seconds. Strain drink into glass through a fine sieve.

3 Pour curaçao and grenadine alternatively into the glass with a spoon to make vertical lines and create a rainbow effect. DO NOT stir or move the glass quickly or the pattern will be distorted.

4 Spear cherry and orange slice on to the cocktail stick and use to decorate glass. Add a short straw before serving.

5 For a less alcoholic drink, omit vodka.

MIXER'S TIP

Keen bartenders can cope with almost anything, except a shortage of ice. If guests are expected, make ice cubes the day before and keep them away from strong-smelling drinks as they easily pick up odours. For clear ice cubes, use boiled or mineral water.

Rainbow Cocktail

Los Angeles

Makes 1 drink

Two cocktails in one; with alcohol it's Los Angeles, without alcohol it's called San Francisco.

1 orange
1 lemon
½ grapefruit
1 tablespoon pineapple juice
1 tablespoon passion fruit juice or peach juice
1 tablespoon grenadine syrup
3 tablespoons vodka
1 tablespoon Grand Marnier
6 ice cubes
1 teaspoon caster sugar

DECORATION
1 long twist of orange peel

EXTRAS
1 tumbler
1 straw

1 Squeeze juice from orange, lemon and grapefruit. Put into a cocktail shaker or thermos flask with pineapple and passion or peach fruit juices and the grenadine syrup.

2 Add vodka, Grand Marnier and 2 ice cubes and shake for 15 seconds.

3 Put the sugar on to a plate. Wipe the rim of the glass with a piece of lemon to moisten. Twist round in the sugar to make a sugary rim.

4 Add rest of ice cubes to glass and then strain in the drink.

5 Hang strip of orange peel over the glass and serve with a straw.

STORM IN A COCKTAIL GLASS - 'HARRYCANE'
Try this exciting new coctail: Put 1 tablespoon malt whisky with 1½ tablespoons cream sherry into a glass. Top up with crushed ice and ginger ale then decorate with a lemon slice.

Los Angeles

Step-by-step

CRUSHING ICE

1 Put ice cubes on to a clean tea-towel and wrap up.

2 Stand on an unbreakable, strong surface and crush with a wooden kitchen mallet until ice breaks down into coarse crystals.

3 Scrape away from tea towel with a scoop and put into a bowl. Leave in freezing compartment of the refrigerator until needed.

FROSTING GLASSES

4 There are two methods to frost glasses. Put the glasses into the deep freeze or freezing compartment of the refrigerator for 1 hour.

5 Alternatively, fill glasses with crushed ice and leave to stand for 5 minutes. Tip out ice.

6 Handle glass with your hand protected by a tea-towel which acts as insulation and stops the "frost" from melting.

TO MAKE SUGAR SYRUP

7 Put 250g (8oz/1 cup) caster sugar into a saucepan with 625ml (1 pint/2½ cups) hot water. Heat slowly, stirring, until sugar dissolves.

8 Brush down sides of pan with a brush dipped in hot water to dissolve sugar crystals.

9 Bring syrup to boil for 1 minute. Remove pan from heat and leave syrup to cool. Leave until cold and then spoon into a bottle through a funnel. Cover and store in a cool place.

1

4

7

2

3

5

6

8

9

Mint Julep

Makes 1 drink

A refreshing combination of mint and bourbon whisky.

5 fresh mint leaves
1 teaspoon icing sugar
2 teaspoons water
6 ice cubes, crushed
1 dash Angostura bitters
4 tablespoons Bourbon whisky

GARNISH
Fresh mint leaves

EXTRAS
1 large tumbler
1 straw

1 Frost the glass following instructions on pages 18 to 19.

2 Put mint leaves into a separate glass or small dish. Add sugar and water and stir briskly with a spoon to bruise leaves.

3 Remove the frosted glass from the refrigerator. Put in the liquid from the mint leaves and then half fill with crushed ice. Add the Angostura and half the Bourbon. Stir to mix.

4 Fill to the rim with more crushed ice and then stir in remaining Bourbon. Decorate with mint and serve with a straw.

WHISKEY KNOW-HOW
Whiskey with an 'ey' at the end comes from Ireland; whisky without the 'e', Scotland. North American whisky - Bourbon - is wheat-based; rye whisky is rye-based; corn whiskey corn-based with a change of spelling at the end to 'ey' as in Irish whiskey.

Mint Julep

Frappé Café de Paris

Makes 2 drinks

An unusually spicy coffee cocktail, enriched with cream and cooled with ice.

625ml (1 pint) extra strong freshly-made coffee
2 cinnamon sticks
4 cloves
4 peppercorns
155ml (¼ pint) whipping cream
6 ice cubes

DECORATION
Powdered drinking chocolate

EXTRAS
1 heatproof jug (minimum 1 litre/1¾ pint/ 4 cups capacity)
2 large glasses, chilled before hand
2 straws

1 Pour hot coffee into the jug and then add cinnamon sticks, cloves and peppercorns.

2 Cover and chill for 1½ hours in the refrigerator.

3 Strain coffee into a blender goblet.

4 Add cream and ice cubes and blend until smooth and foamy.

5 Pour into 2 glasses and sprinkle tops with drinking chocolate. Add a straw to each and drink while still foamy.

MIXER'S TIP
Drinks blended with crushed ice, known as frappé, are wonderfully cooling and are composed of alcoholic drinks or fruit nectars poured into glasses filled with crushed ice. Favourites for frappé drinks are Tia Maria (Tia Maria Frappé), Creme de Menthe, Cassis, grenadine syrup, and for nonalcoholic versions, fruit nectars or fruit juice.

Frappé Café de Paris

Champagne Cocktail

Makes 1 drink

The perfect cocktail for celebrations.

155ml (5fl oz/⅔ cup) champagne (or sparkling wine)
1 sugar cube
1 dash of Angostura bitters
1 tablespoon brandy

EXTRAS
1 champagne flute

1 Chill the champagne or sparkling wine in its bottle. Chill the glass at the same time.

2 Before serving, put the sugar into the chilled glass. Add Angostura and brandy.

3 Fill the glass with the champagne or sparkling wine and serve straight away.

BLACK VELVET
A slick smoothie, made from Guinness and Champagne mixed half and half; daring perhaps but masterful and memorable. Try this: Half fill a large wine glass SLOWLY with Guinness so that it keeps its head. Top up gradually with chilled champagne and serve straight away.

Champagne Cocktail

Green Fizz

Makes 1 drink

A stunning new cocktail, laced with peppermint liqueur.

1 egg white
Crushed ice
Juice of ½ lemon
1 teaspoon icing sugar
3 tablespoons gin or vodka
1 teaspoon Crème de Menthe (green peppermint liqueur)
Sparkling mineral water

DECORATION

1 slice lemon

EXTRAS

1 large tumbler
1 straw

1 Pour egg white into cocktail shaker or thermos flask.

2 Fill glass with crushed ice.

3 Add lemon juice, icing sugar, gin or vodka and Crème de Menthe to egg white in shaker or flask and shake briskly for 15 seconds.

4 Strain drink into glass over ice and then top up with mineral water.

5 Decorate with lemon slice and add a straw before serving.

FIZZ AND FANTASY

Fizz is a colloquial name for an assortment of classic cocktails such as Buck's Fizz or Gin Fizz. To make traditional Gin Fizz, put a teaspoon of icing sugar or sugar syrup (see pages 18-19) into a cocktail shaker or thermos flask. Add the juice of a lemon, 3 tablespoons gin and about 6 ice cubes. Shake rhythmically for 10-15 seconds. Strain into a tumbler, filled with crushed ice.

Green Fizz

Tom Collins

Makes 1 drink

A fresh-tasting cocktail from North America.

4 ice cubes
1 lemon
75ml (2½fl oz) gin
1 teaspoon icing sugar or sugar syrup
Sparkling mineral water

DECORATION
1 cocktail cherry
1 slice orange

EXTRAS
1 tall tumbler
1 straw

1 Put ice cubes into a cocktail shaker or thermos flask.

2 Halve lemon, cut off a thin slice and keep for decoration. Squeeze juice from both lemon halves and pour over the ice cubes.

3 Add the gin and the icing sugar or sugar syrup.

4 Shake briskly for 20 seconds.

5 Strain drink into glass through a sieve.

6 Top up with mineral water to within 2.5cm (1in) of rim of glass.

7 Decorate with the cocktail cherry, orange and reserved lemon slice. Add a straw to serve.

MIXER'S TIPS
Try the Tom Collins with whisky, Cognac or tequila instead of gin. Substitute lime for lemon to make Gimlet, or for a classic Daiquiri, use lemonade instead of mineral water and white rum for gin.

Tom Collins

Piña Colada

Makes 1 drink

A tropical, all time favourite.

4 ice cubes
3 tablespoons pineapple juice
3 tablespoons white rum
30g (1oz) creamed coconut, coarsely grated or cut into small pieces

DECORATION

1 cocktail cherry
1 piece of unpeeled pineapple

EXTRAS

1 medium tumbler, chilled beforehand
1 decorative cocktail stick
1 straw

1 Put the ice cubes and pineapple juice into a cocktail shaker or thermos flask.

2 Add the rum together with the creamed coconut.

3 Shake drink briskly for 15 seconds and then strain through a sieve into glass.

4 Spear the cherry and piece of pineapple on to a cocktail stick and stand on top of the glass. Add straw.

MAKING COCONUT MILK

Nothing can equal fresh coconut milk in a Pina Colada. To make, puncture the coconut in the 2 places where the 'eyes' are situated and drain the liquid (the milk) into a bowl. Break open the coconut, take away the hard shell and grate the flesh on to a plate. Add to the coconut milk with 315ml (½ pint/1¼ cups) boiling water. Leave to stand for 1 hour. Drain through a fine sieve into a large jug, pressing grated coconut against sides of sieve to remove as much liquid as possible. Pour into a jar or bottle with a tight-fitting stopper. Chill for up to 3 days. Use 4 tablespoons for every Pina Colada.

Piña Colada

Sangria

Serves 6

A refreshing but potent Spanish drink made from red wine, brandy and orange liqueur.

4 lemons
1 orange
2 fresh peaches or 440g (14oz) can peach slices in natural juice
1 litre (1¾ pints/4 cups) Spanish red wine
75ml (2½fl oz/⅓ cup) brandy
3 tablespoons Cointreau or Curaçao
2 tablespoons caster sugar
3 cloves, optional

EXTRAS

1 large jug or carafe, about 2 litres or 3½ pints/8 cups) in capacity

1 Squeeze the juice from 3 lemons. Slice remaining lemon and the orange.

2 If using fresh peaches, peel and wash and cut flesh into thin slices.

3 Pour the wine into a large jug and then add brandy, Cointreau or Curaçao and sugar. Stir until sugar has completely dissolved. Add cloves, if using.

4 Add the peach slices or drained canned peaches and the orange and lemon slices. Stir, cover and chill a minimum of at least 4 hours in the refrigerator. If the Sangria seems on the strong side, dilute to taste with sparkling mineral water or lemonade.

CUPS LIKE SANGRIA

You can vary the ingredients for Sangria according to taste or availability. Use fruit preserved in alcohol instead of peach slices; honey instead of sugar; and sparkling white wine instead of mineral water or lemonade. Stand the jug in a bowl of crushed ice to keep the Sangria cool or pour into an insulated jug.

Sangria